A 25-Day Countdown To Christmas

Devotions and Poems for Those Caught
Between Snowflakes and Schedules

Pam Kumpe

Scripture quotations from the ESV Bible, The Holy Bible, English Standard Version, copyright 2001 by Crossway Bibles, a publishing ministry of Good News Publishers.

Used by permission. All rights reserved.

No part of this publication may be reproduced, distributed, or transmitted in any form or by any means or stored in a database or retrieval system without prior written permission of the publisher. All rights reserved.

Cover Design by: Pam Kumpe

Copyright 2025 Pam Kumpe

ISBN 979-8-9921326-6-3

Pam Kumpe

This book is dedicated to my late earthly father, W.C. Dunn—the man who handed out church bulletins like tiny gifts of grace. Your smile welcomed strangers. Your obedience honored the One you loved. Your quiet loyalty to Jesus echoed through every life you touched. This Christmas—and always—your legacy shines brighter than any star on any tree.

December 1
Wonderful Counselor

"For to us a child is born, to us a son is given; and the government shall be upon his shoulder, and his name shall be called Wonderful Counselor, Mighty God, Everlasting Father, Prince of Peace."
Isaiah 9:6, ESV

Let's be honest—sometimes my thoughts look like a pile of Christmas lights stuffed in a box since last year. They're tangled, not flashing, and I may appear like I have no idea how to get ready for the holiday. But Jesus, the Wonderful Counselor, steps right into that mental and emotional clutter with gentleness.

He doesn't frown and shake His head—He kneels beside us with patience.

When my heart races to fix things or to figure it all out, He reminds me: *You don't have to carry every answer, because you know the One who does.*

He's not just wonderful because He's wise. He's wonderful because He's willing to meet us in the confusion, or in the ongoing busyness of December, as we make plans for holiday parties, family events, caroling, church, shopping, and baking.

The Counselor listens when words fail, when delays happen, when plans dissolve like sugar in a cake mix.

He guides when logic folds. He steadies when our confidence wobbles, when our dreams stall, when we wonder.

Maybe today you just need to exhale and whisper, *"Lord, help me untangle this mess."* He will, every time. Because He's not only the Wonderful Counselor—He's the patient One who stays until peace returns.

"At the Sea of Galilee"

He strolled along the water's edge,
no clipboard, no stern face.
Just the kind of calm you notice
when chaos is out of place.

Fishermen fumbled with broken nets,
their night's work nearly gone.
But He tossed them words of wisdom
and the courage to cast on.

The wind took notes, the waves stood still,
and even seagulls seemed to pause.
Because creation knew His voice
belonged to more than laws.

"Try again," Jesus said with a grin,
and nets came back alive with grace.
They didn't just catch fish.
They caught hope, see it in their face.

The shoreline hummed with holy hush,
as peace replaced their fear.
The Sea of Galilee still tells the tale,
the Wonderful Counselor was here.

Prayer

Jesus, step into my thoughts today. Untangle what's knotted and quiet what's loud. Guide me with Your wisdom and remind me I don't walk alone. Amen

December 2
Prince of Peace

*"For He Himself is our peace, who has made us both one and has broken down in His flesh
the dividing wall of hostility."*
Ephesians 2:14, ESV

If peace were a feeling, we'd spend our lives chasing it like the last parking spot at Walmart on Christmas Eve. But peace, real peace, is not a mood—it's a Person. And His name is Jesus.

The world shouts, and you tell yourself, "Calm down!" while Jesus whispers, "Come close."

Chaos sets up camp like packed leftovers from your Christmas meal and plans to stay forever, but Jesus walks right through the middle of it, not with panic, not with force, but with authority stronger than any storm. Stronger than the scent of cranberry sauce on your dressing flavored with way too much sage.

When your thoughts feel like they're doing backflips, or when your tickertape of worry won't hush even when you're exhausted, Jesus says, *"My peace isn't earned, it's given. My peace isn't temporary; it's eternal. My peace isn't fragile, it's unshakeable."*

So today, instead of trying to *find* peace like it's hiding behind the couch cushions, *receive* it from the One who carries it, owns it, and offers it freely.

Real peace doesn't depend on your circumstances, behavior, or the challenge of not overeating at your Christmas meal; nor does it lie in the idea that wrapping the perfect gift for someone is the answer.

It depends on who you're walking with. Hold His hand. The Prince of Peace is your strength during the holiday shuffle and the mincemeat and pralines.

The calm we long for is within reach, and He will soothe our hearts. Jesus is the Prince of Peace. Always.

"On the Mount of Beatitudes"

He climbed the hill where anxious hearts
gathered like sheep needing rest,
and He spoke of peace not borrowed
but peace He carried in His chest.

The breeze leaned in to hear Him speak,
birds stopped mid-flight to catch His tone,
for Heaven whispered through His voice:
"You never have to stand alone."

"Blessed are the peace-receivers,
and blessed are the peacemakers, too,
for My peace isn't just a Sunday thought
it walks daily along with you."

And still that hillside calls us back,
like an echo carved in holy stone:
The Prince of Peace walks with you now
you're never fighting storms alone.

Even if your holiday shopping chases you.

Prayer

Lord, speak Your peace over my heart. Calm every anxious place and steady every shaky breath. Fill me with Your stillness today. Amen.

December 3
Light of the World

"Again, Jesus spoke to them, saying, 'I am the light of the world. Whoever follows Me will not walk in darkness but will have the light of life.'"
John 8:12, ESV

Darkness is loud. It whispers worst-case scenarios, spotlights our insecurities, and tries to convince us that shadows have more authority than they really do.

And the hope of Christmas can become lost in our lists, chores, and the bustle of running to and from the stores with coupons for this, rewards cash for that, and sales galore, only to stress when a light at an intersection makes us sit too long.

But Jesus doesn't fight darkness with more noise—He arrives, and darkness loses its job.

His light isn't like the kind that flickers when the power goes out or fades when we're tired. His light is steady, warm, and bold enough to reach the corners we pretend don't exist.

And when Jesus shines, He doesn't shame us—He reveals truth kindly, guides gently, and brings clarity where confusion once camped out. His light helps our steps make sense again.

So, the next time you stop at a red light, remember the caution before the red: slow down, take a pause, and toss the unimportant from your day.

Today, if life feels dim or heavy, whisper: *"Jesus, shine here. I need you. Ride with me. I can't do this alone."*

And He will.

Because light doesn't strain to win over darkness—it just shows up, and darkness scatters. However, be cautious, as the other drivers may also need the light you seek.

Don't let them dent your heart or your car.

So, as you drive, enter all intersections of the day with Jesus by your side. And watch His light give way to joy.

"In the Temple Courts"

Lampstands flickered in the crowded court,
shadows dancing on ancient stone,
while weary souls lingered in the dark,
feeling small, unseen, unknown.

Then Jesus spoke—
and darkness fled,
hope rose,
light spread.

His words cut through the heaviness,
like morning slipping past the night,
reminding every watching heart:
you were made to walk in light.

Where His voice falls, shadows surrender,
fear retreats, and faith takes a view.
The Light of the World still shines today—
on you, in you, for you.

Follow Jesus. And move along with hope.

Prayer

Jesus, shine Your light into every corner of my life. Chase away the shadows, brighten my steps, and help me walk with confidence in Your truth. Amen.

December 4
Good Shepherd

> *"I am the good shepherd. The good shepherd lays down his life for the sheep."*
> John 10:11, ESV

If we're honest, we don't always wander because we're rebellious; sometimes we wander because we're tired, distracted, hurting, curious, or convinced we can handle life with our own personal "Do It Your Way Survival kit."

But the Good Shepherd knows every slope, valley, pit, thorn, and cliff. He's not surprised when we slip. He's prepared.

He doesn't holler from a distance like an annoyed supervisor. Or shout over the intercom of a store you've stayed in too long, where you're caught in lines, shopping for pie crust, or pumpkin filling, or candy canes on aisle three.

He comes close. He rescues, not scolds. He carries, not critiques. His shoulders have been proven strong enough for lost, limping, confused sheep, and that includes the moments when we aren't even sure *how* we got lost in the first place.

And when He calls your name, it's not a roll call—it's an invitation.

So, as you walk today. Whether shopping. Strolling. Or wishing you had the money to touch a life with a gift you can't buy this year; take time to tune your ears to the One voice that never leads you wrong.

Some of you have an abundance. Others wish for more.

But remember, love isn't found in aisle three or four of the holiday section or through that mall door. It's found in your Good Shepherd.

He is coming for you—and for all. And that's a gift you can share, that costs you nothing, except your time.

Jesus is the best present you can offer someone.

"In the Judean Hills"

Across the rugged, restless hills
where shepherds walked beneath the stars,
Jesus spoke of a Shepherd brave
who'd chase the lost no matter how far.

He knows the landscape of your heart,
its hidden valleys, shadowed frame.
The Judean hills still echo loudly:
He calls you by your truest name.

His rescue is not hesitant,
nor based on worth or strength or whim.
The hills declare with sacred wind:
no sheep is *ever* lost to Him.

And He calls to you, with a love so deep.
Say yes and run to Him.

Prayer

Shepherd of my soul, call my name and I will follow. Lead me where I need to go, carry me when I'm weak, and keep me close to Your heart. Amen.

December 5
Bread of Life

"Jesus said to them, 'I am the bread of life; whoever comes to Me shall not hunger, and whoever believes in Me shall never thirst.'"
John 6:35, ESV

We all know what physical hunger feels like—stomach grumbling, mind wandering, patience evaporating.

Still, there's a deeper hunger that snacks, success, social media, relationships, accomplishments, Christmas parties, or even ministry can't satisfy, nor can turkey, sausage balls, or fudge.

It's that hunger underneath the surface—the longing for meaning, belonging, reassurance, and identity.

And Jesus doesn't offer a quick snack of comfort like pecan pie or sugar cookies sprinkled with green sugar.

He offers Himself.

He isn't the supplement of life—He is the Sustainer.

He isn't the side dish, like green bean casserole, either. Or mac and cheese. Or yeast rolls.

He is the source of everything. He is the feast that fills forever—the main portion.

So, if your soul feels thin today—tired, overlooked, stretched, or aching, sit, breathe slowly, and feast on His presence.

You don't have to earn a seat.

You're already invited.

Open your Bible. Walk through the gospels. Take in the birth of the Savior. Meet His mother. His father. And absorb the scriptures before you.

Accept the call as Jesus fills your life with Himself. Your name card at the table awaits. Let Christ write your name in His Book of Life.

"In the Synagogue at Capernaum"

People gathered hungry
not for bread, but for answers,
carrying questions like empty baskets
and hearts that needed more than grain.

Jesus offered Himself instead—
not a lesson, not a lecture,
but the Living Bread.
That never molds, never spoils,
never runs out when life gets thin.

Bread that fills what emptiness drains.
Bread that strengthens what struggle weakens.
Bread that satisfies what nothing else can,
not applause, not achievement,
not even the best "good day."

Capernaum still remembers His claim,
spoken bold beneath stone and scroll.
And somewhere deep within your heart
those same words echo, warm and whole:
The Bread of Life still feeds the soul.

Prayer

Lord, nourish what is hungry in me. Feed my spirit with You and satisfy the places nothing else can fill. Amen.

December 6
Emmanuel (God with Us)

"Behold, the virgin shall conceive and bear a son, and they shall call His name Immanuel" (which means, God with us). Matthew 1:23, ESV

There's something breathtaking about the words "God with us." He's not near us in theory. Not watching from a safe distance with Heavenly binoculars. With us!

He's not checking to see if we've been bad or good. Or to see if we've accomplished our holiday lists and wrapped all our gifts with matching bows. Or making sure you've made your sausage balls.

He is with us. Emmanuel.

With us in joy that bubbles over. With us in grief that feels too heavy to name. With us in faith that's strong, and with us, that's held together by faith, bound by Heavenly duct tape and late-night prayers.

Emmanuel doesn't wait for us to *feel* holy, *act* collected, or *pretend* to be brave. He steps right into the ordinary moments most people scroll past: the drive-thru lane, the messy living room, the flour on the counter, the pine needles on the floor from the fresh-cut Christmas tree.

He's there on the lonely car ride, when you miss family in another state, and the silent "Lord, please help me," whispered into a pillow. You don't have to climb a spiritual ladder to reach Him.

He came down every rung to reach you. So go ahead... Sweep up the pine needles. Finish those sausage balls. And wipe the counter and rid yourself of that overwhelming worry, grief, or loneliness.

And whisper this, like medicine to your soul: *I am not alone. He is with me. With me.*

"In Nazareth"

Nazareth was small,
a hillside town of dust and chatter,
nothing postcard-pretty,
nothing people thought would matter.

Yet Heaven placed its footprint there,
where life was plain, unseen, and slow.
Because Emmanuel writes holy things
in places where we'd never go.

He still chooses unlikely corners:
your worn-out sighs, your hidden tears,
your Wednesday worries tucked away,
your calendar full of ordinary years.

He enters rooms without applause,
sits quietly where doubts rebel,
and whispers through the heavy air:
"I didn't come to impress... I came to dwell."

Not distant. Not formal.
not visiting just on holidays,
but close enough to breathe your air
and stay with you in all your ways.

Prayer

God with us, remind my heart that You are here. Stay close in every joy and sit with me in every sorrow. Let Your presence be my peace. Amen.

December 7
Lamb of God

"The next day he saw Jesus coming toward him, and said, 'Behold, the Lamb of God, who takes away the sin of the world!'"
John 1:29, ESV

The *Lamb of God* didn't come wrapped in soft poetry or sweet sentiment. He came with the weight of rescue and the price of redemption. Lambs were familiar to the people who heard it, but this *Lamb* was different. He didn't come to be observed... He came to be offered.

He didn't shy away from the mess of humanity. He took it upon Himself. Every regret, every failure, every misstep, every "I wish I could take that back,' and He came for our sins. He carried them to the cross not reluctantly, not resentfully, but willingly.

Jesus, the Lamb of God, didn't die because we were lovable; He died because we were loved.

And when shame tries to rewrite your identity or replay your worst scenes, remember, forgiven is not your *grade,* it's your *birthright* in Christ.

You don't have to earn what He already paid for. You don't have to fix what He already finished. Redemption is not a reward—it's a gift.

So today, let grace be the loudest voice in the room. Decorate the day with hope in Christ. You are covered. You are His.

With the Christmas list growing. With the dates blocked off for parties. With the day calling your name.

Take time. Hit pause. Slow down. And have a sweet talk with the *Lamb*. Remember, Candy canes are sweet. But Jesus is sweeter. Regret may knock on your heart this Christmas; however, the Lamb restores. And makes all things new.

"*In Bethany*"

Bethany felt like the kind of town
where friendship softened every day,
where laughter lingered in the air
and love refused to fade away.

Jesus paused there on His journey,
not to rush or to conceal
but to show that sacred purpose
can walk hand in hand with what is real.

He knew a cross lay just ahead,
He knew what perfect love would cost,
yet shared His heart in Bethany
to prove no broken soul is lost.

The Lamb of God walked toward His fate
not forced, not trapped, not pushed or grim
but led by love so fierce and full
He'd give His life for *them*—and *us*.

And when regret tries knocking loud,
Bethany whispers softly within:
The Lamb who died and rose again
declares you clean, restored, and His.

Prayer

Jesus, thank You for taking what I could not carry. Cover me again in Your grace, cleanse my heart, and help me live in the freedom You paid for. Amen.

December 8
Redeemer

"For I know that my Redeemer lives, and at the last He will stand upon the earth."
Job 19:25, ESV

There's something breathtaking about the word Redeemer, a reminder that *nothing about your life is wasted*. Not the tears, not the waiting, not the years you thought were ruined, nor the pages you wish you could rewrite. God doesn't hand out "replacement stories." He *redeems* the one you have.

Your life may seem like a Christmas tree filled with ornaments representing various seasons, including those of crisis, despair, joy, and merriment. All mixed together. All a part of who you are.

Redeeming isn't the same as denying hurt—it's declaring that hurt won't have the final vote.

Maybe you've lived through seasons that looked like a spiritual yard sale: pieces everywhere, value unclear, and a story that felt like it needed a "free to a good home" sign. But the Redeemer doesn't bargain or bargain-hunt; He *restores what is priceless*.

He doesn't just pull you from the rubble, He builds something meaningful right where the dust still settles. And the best part? Your Redeemer lives. That means hope does, too.

So today, when old memories knock or discouragement whispers, answer back and say it with grace: *"This chapter isn't over. My Redeemer is still writing."*

Your Christmas memory is ahead. What will it say? What will you pray? And who will remember your kindness or smile?

The Redeemer is writing perfection on your walk with Him. May it add a spice of encouragement to others along the way.

"At the Jordan River"

The riverbank held whispered prayers,
where wanderers washed dust away,
and voices echoed through
the reeds of second chances on display.

Then Jesus stepped into the stream,
not needing cleansing of His own,
but choosing solidarity with hearts
that felt too heavy-grown.

The Jordan carried stories past
of battles fought and sins confessed.
Yet when the Redeemer touched its waves,
the water *learned* what grace looked best.

He steps inside our murky parts,
where guilt and shame
once pooled to the brim,
and wades through all we cannot fix
till what was lost is found *in Him*.

Prayer

Redeemer, take what feels broken in me and make it whole.
Rewrite my story with Your mercy and redeem
what I cannot fix. Amen.

December 9
Alpha and Omega

"'I am the Alpha and the Omega,' says the Lord God, 'who is and who was and who is to come, the Almighty.'" Revelation 1:8, ESV

Life has a way of handing us chapters we didn't plan for and Grinch-like twists we didn't audition for. Some beginnings feel exciting, others feel overwhelming. Some endings are celebrated, others leave us crying in the shower, wondering if there's anything good ahead.

But Jesus declares something powerful over every timeline: I am the First Word and the Final Say.

He was there before your story began, before the scars, before the sharp turns, before the fear. And He will be there long after the tinsel falls from the Christmas tree, or the things that keep you up at night.

Your joy doesn't depend on luck, timing, or perfect decisions; it rests in the Author whose ink never runs dry.

He doesn't panic when the toy you went after is already out of stock. He doesn't scrap the hope, because most of your family won't make it home for the holiday. He doesn't ghost you when your reactions aren't pretty, or when the tears come from the pressure and conflict rises.

So, whether you're in the phase of burning the cake, dropping the hot chocolate, or forgetting the sage for the chicken and dressing, remember that the One who came in a manger is already sitting at the table, holding victory in His hands.

No season surprises Him. No spills. No burnt food, no turning point makes him forget you either. No moment you face will ever intimidate Christ. Just hold onto Him.

He is the Alpha. He is the Omega. And He is beautifully faithful in everything between.

Pour yourself some apple cider. Sip on it. Enjoy the flavor. And let Christmas mean more to you than it ever has before. Share a moment with the Savior each day. And breathe.

"On the Mount of Transfiguration"

Glory wrapped Him like lightning's robe,
as time knelt still beneath His feet,
with Moses standing on one side
and fire-eyed Elijah at His seat.

Past and promise shared the mountain,
history hushed to hear His claim
eternity breathed through His presence
as Heaven whispered out His Name.

Alpha—older than dawn's first light,
Omega—Author of every end,
He stood unchanged while ages bowed,
not distant God, but trusted Friend.

So, when your plans twist with fear,
or the pressure feels too steep to climb,
remember mountains still proclaim:
He holds your first breath *and* your time.

Prayer

Lord, I know you hold my beginnings and my endings. Give me faith to trust Your timeline right now in the middle, and the courage to follow Your lead. Amen.

December 10
Savior

> *"For unto you is born this day in the city of David a Savior, who is Christ the Lord."*
> Luke 2:11, ESV

We often picture the word Savior in gold script on Christmas cards, framed with snowflakes and soft candlelight. We place those cards on mantles and enjoy them for the whole month.

But the need for a Savior isn't poetic; it's urgent, personal, and real.

We don't need saving because we're weak failures—we need saving because we're human beings living in a broken world with hearts that bend, bruise, and sometimes bolt in the wrong direction.

Our gold script of choices can go every which way, and then we lose our reason for celebrating Christmas when the blur of rushing takes over.

And Jesus didn't become Savior from a distance. He stepped into the very world that needed saving—not as a warrior with flashing armor, but as a baby wrapped in humility and held by human arms.

He saves us from sin, yes, but also from despair, from shame, from self-reliance that crumbles, and from the lie that Christmas requires more wrapping paper, more fudge, more toys, and more gifts.

You don't have to climb up to be rescued. The Savior is reaching for your heart and your hand.

So today, instead of trying harder, checking sales, getting in those long lines, or buying one more item, maybe whisper: *"Jesus, save me from myself."*

And remember, that's a prayer He always answers with love. In gold script that says, *"Yes, you are mine."*

"In Bethlehem's Fields"

Shepherds watched their flocks that night
beneath a sky too dark to see,
until the heavens broke in song
and glory spilled across the sea.

Angels sang of saving grace,
their voices bright as morning gold—
"Your Savior's come, go find Him now!"
In tones both fearless and so bold.

They ran with ragged hope aflame,
hearts pounding fast with joy untamed,
for rescue came in swaddled cloth,
in stable air unashamed.

And Bethlehem still hums with truth
in the manger dust and whispered hymns.
Our Savior didn't need a throne.
He came to dwell with us...

Because the Savior lives.

Prayer

Jesus, save me from today—save my thoughts, my choices, my heart, and my moments. Thank You for rescuing me with love that never quits. Amen.

December 11
King of Kings

"On His robe and on His thigh, He has a name written, King of kings and Lord of lords."
Revelation 19:16, ESV

Most kings rise to power by climbing ladders, winning battles, or inheriting a throne. But Jesus didn't fight His way to royalty. He *is* royalty.

His crown wasn't earned by domination, fear, armies, or politics. He wore a crown of thorns before He ever revealed His crown of glory. What kind of King does that?

The king who isn't insecure. The king who doesn't need a palace to be powerful. The king who bends low to lift His people high. The king who conquers not with weapons, but with love stronger than death.

King of kings means:

- no power outranks Him
- no authority intimidates Him
- no darkness overrules Him
- no enemy overthrows Him

When life feels out of control this December, remember the King is not pacing Heaven's halls wringing His hands.

He is seated. Steady. Sovereign. Present. Kind.

And best of all? You are not merely *under* His rule... His care holds you.

Never forget. Jesus rules the world with truth and grace and righteousness—a wonder of His love to behold.

At Christmas. And throughout the year!

He is the King of kings.

"At the Southern Steps of the Temple"

Kings are known for marble gates,
for guards and gold and guarded halls,
for towering thrones and royal feasts
and echoes down their hallowed walls.

But Jesus walked where sandals scraped,
where common dust kissed common feet,
and chose the temple's southern steps
instead of polished royal seats.

He taught with power, calm, and grace,
no scepter, crown, or jeweled ring.
Yet hearts bowed low in trembling awe
before the world's true, humble King.

And still those ancient steps proclaim
through whispered wind and history's call:
the King of kings walks with His own,
not far above, but with us all.

Prayer

My King, rule in my heart and reign in my decisions. Help me trust Your authority and rest beneath Your care. Amen.

December 12
The Door

"I am the door. If anyone enters by Me, he will be saved and will go in and out and find pasture."
John 10:9, ESV

When Jesus calls Himself *The Door*, He isn't referring to a locked entry only accessible to the elite, the well-behaved, or the spiritually flawless.

He's not a "secret passageway" hidden behind religious achievement either. He is the wide-open, grace-built, always-accessible entrance into life, belonging, and rest.

And unlike the doors we've all experienced:

- He doesn't slam shut when we stumble
- He doesn't creak closed with conditions
- He doesn't require a perfect password
- He doesn't swing open only for those who "look the part."

No. He is The Door that stays open because His love stays open to use. He never changes, even when we get caught up in the hustle and bustle of overdoing it at Christmas.

When guilt tries to convince you that you don't get to come close, Jesus gently reminds you that He Himself *is* the way inside—not your performance, not your spiritual highlight reel. Not the partridge in the pear tree, you had to have, or the drummers drumming toy set.

If you've ever felt like you didn't belong, like you were one step outside of "enough," or like life had too many closed doors... Jesus stands there with His hand extended and His heart wide.

You don't have to knock loudly. You don't have to bargain. You just come, and He welcomes you.

Keep close to Him, though, because the call of Christmas has many doors. And the only one you need is the door that leads to Jesus.

"By the Sheep Gate"

The Sheep Gate wasn't fancy built,
nor lined with gold or praised by men,
it smelled of flocks and sacrifice
and all that felt too "less than."

But Jesus stood beside that gate,
declaring words both bold and sure:
"I am the Door—come enter in,
and find your rest, your safety, your cure."

No velvet ropes, no guarded guards,
no whispered, "You don't qualify."
Just open grace where broken hearts
walk in and finally breathe and sigh.

And still the ancient stones retell
what weary souls can't yet ignore:
for all who feel locked out by life—
Jesus remains the welcome Door.

Walk in.

Prayer

Jesus, open the right doors and close the wrong ones. Lead me through the places You've prepared and help me walk boldly into Your will. Amen.

December 13
The Vine

"I am the vine; you are the branches. Whoever abides in Me and I in him, he it is that bears much fruit, for apart from Me you can do nothing."
John 15:5, ESV

Trying to live strong without staying connected to Jesus is like sticking a cut flower in a vase and expecting it to grow roots. It might *look* okay for a little while, but eventually beauty fades, strength wilts, and life can become hard to sustain.

Jesus didn't say, "Try harder. Hustle more. Impress Me." He said, "Abide."

Which means:

- stay close
- stay connected
- stay dependent
- stay with Me

Fruit isn't produced by effort but by attachment. Love, joy, peace, patience, kindness, goodness, faithfulness, gentleness, and self-control aren't traits we *manufacture*—they are evidence of a life rooted in Christ.

So, if you're weary this December, don't assume you've failed; it may just be time to stop striving and rest your soul in Him again.

He is the Vine that never dries out, never breaks, never withers, and never stops giving life to those who stay close.

On days ahead, when you buy seven packs of wrapping paper, two snowman globes for your friends, and a gingerbread yard ornament that lights up, remember that abiding in Christ requires more than a tap on your phone's app to read the verse of the day.

Abiding means your *heart* remains close to Christ, even if the wrapping paper was 75% off.

"Among the Vineyard Terraces"

Terraced hills rose like ancient steps,
where grapevines curled through dust and stone,
and clusters grew not by their strength
but by the Vine's strength alone.

Branches never strained to bloom,
nor wrestled fruit from stubborn air
they simply clung with quiet trust,
and found their fullness growing there.

No self-made fruit, no hurried proof,
no frantic grasp for worth or win
just life that dripped from sacred roots
and flowed like grace through branch and limb.

Still vineyards hum this gentle truth
for hearts worn thin and stretched in twine:
real growth begins where striving ends
and souls rest deep within the Vine.

Prayer

Lord, keep me connected to You. Strengthen me, grow Your fruit in me, and teach me to rest in You. Help me stay connected and dependent on You. Amen.

December 14
Rock of Ages

"He alone is my rock and my salvation, my fortress;
I shall not be greatly shaken."
Psalm 62:2, ESV

Some days, life feels steady, and other days feel like the ground beneath us shifts without warning. Plans crumble, people change, emotions wobble, and suddenly we're gripping hope like it's slipping through our fingers.

But when Scripture calls Jesus our Rock, it's not describing a pebble we keep in our pocket for inspiration—it's telling the immovable, unshakeable, weather-proof foundation of our lives.

Jesus is that Rock that doesn't crack under pressure or erode when storms hit, or crumble under the weight of our questions, or shift when you're missing someone this month and nostalgia squeezes hard.

December can feel overwhelming as you face crowded stores, parking lot battles, lost items, or family expectations. And those things can roar louder than faith, as if we're facing a spiritual earthquake, but remember, Jesus remains steady.

Your emotions may shake, but your foundation won't. Your future may feel uncertain, but your Savior knows what's ahead. And your knees may tremble, but your Rock will not move.

And sometimes the greatest act of faith is to plant both feet and whisper... "I trust You, even here."

So, when school parties, church programs, and work gatherings happen, all on a Monday, speak to the Rock.

He listens. He hears. He holds. He calms. He consoles.

Let Him know you need to be pulled close and quieted, as you long for peace that will outshine the noise.

For many, sanity is required to get through this month, and He's the answer to your call, to keep you from falling.

"At the Cliffs of Arbel (Hosea 10)"

The cliffs stood tall above the land,
carved deep by wind and storm-torn years,
yet never bowed to thunder's roar
nor shrank beneath the sky's wild tears.

Their rugged strength told ancient tales
of weathered nights and brutal tests,
but still they towered, firm and sure,
unmoved, unbroken, steadfast, blessed.

So too, our Rock—no shifting sand,
no fragile hope that bends or breaks;
He steadies hearts through crashing waves
and holds us firm when whole worlds shake.

And the Lord whispers still to souls
who fear their strength is wearing thin:
your Rock is greater than the storm
lean hard and rest your weight on Him.

He will keep you steady.

Prayer

Jesus, be my steady place. Anchor my heart when fear rises and keep me grounded in Your unshakable love. Amen.

December 15
Messiah

"He first found his own brother Simon and said to him, 'We have found the Messiah.'"
John 1:41, ESV

The word Messiah wasn't casual; it was the longing of generations, the heartbeat of prophecy, the hope whispered by weary souls who wondered if rescue would ever really come.

Messiah meant *promised One*, the One who carries God's rescue plan, mercy plan, and redemption plan all wrapped up in Himself.

The Messiah didn't arrive with headlines, parades, or palace invitations. He came quietly—not to impress, but to fulfill.

And what He fulfills, He completes. What He promises, He performs. What He begins, He perfects.

People spend their lives searching for "the thing" that will finally fix what hurts, quiet what screams, fill what aches, heal what's broken, or answer what confuses.

But *the thing* we need has never been a thing—it has always been a Person. And when the Messiah steps into your life, He doesn't just change what you *do*... He changes what you *believe is possible*.

At times, maybe you've found yourself believing Christmas was powered by sugar cookies, full shopping carts, and matching pajamas, or synchronized twinkle lights.

And then you step outside one night, and a snowflake hits your eyelashes like glitter from Heaven, and you find yourself asking. "Jesus, is Christmas supposed to feel like this?"

We already know the answer.

Jesus didn't come to boost a holiday; He came to transform souls. Christmas isn't something we buy. It's Someone we believe and love.

"On Jacob's Well Road (Sychar)"

A weary woman met Him there,
where noonday sun burned hot and wide,
and tried to hide her tangled past
behind a jar and humbled pride.

But Messiah doesn't flinch or fade,
nor step back from the truth we bear;
He speaks of water deep and free,
and hope that overflows despair.

Her shame-filled story met His grace
and what she carried lost its sting;
she left her jar but gained new life,
and she ran, telling the town and well, and spring.

Still, Jacob's road sings soft with air,
where dust meets love and truth meets fear:
the Messiah builds new stories
from the ones we thought unclear.

Prayer

Messiah, fulfill Your purpose in me. Heal my heart, strengthen my faith, and help me walk into the hope You bring. Rescue me from the rush of the holiday. Amen.

December 16
The Word

"In the beginning was the Word, and the Word was with God, and the Word was God."
John 1:1, ESV

Words matter. They build or break, soothe or sting, restore or ruin. But when Scripture calls Jesus The Word, it means He is *God's full message*, God's clearest communication, God's heart expressed in human form.

He didn't come merely to *explain* God to people; He came to *reveal* Him to us, to invite us to know the Savior.

Every time Jesus spoke, healed, forgave, touched, welcomed, challenged, or restored, God Himself was speaking through Him. He became the living translation of divine love into everyday human language.

So, when questions rise like waves, and your answers don't show up in bigger lights, bigger gifts, or bigger plans, remember bigger isn't necessarily better.

Once, I heard an elderly woman behind me at church singing "O Come Let Us Adore Him," and her voice was low; she wasn't trying to impress; she was inviting the Savior into her song and her life.

So, friend, if you're chasing the sparkle instead of the Savior, think of this woman. She led a quiet life, and her faith shone brighter than any rooftop display, one that will never burn out.

And if you're living in the bigger and louder part of the holiday, and things seem confusing and you need clarity, or when you wish

Heaven would speak louder, you don't have to strain to find answers. Look at Jesus —He is the Word that makes God known.

The Word still lives. The Word still speaks. The Word still saves. The Word is always better. And in this case, so much bigger than anything.

"In the Nazareth Synagogue"

The scroll was spread with careful hands,
inked lines of truth and history's sigh,
as villagers leaned in to hear
their ancient hope sang through the sky.

He read the words Isaiah penned,
yet spoke as if those lines were flame
the prophecy stood up alive,
and wrapped itself around His Name.

The Word read *the* Word with steady breath,
not distant, vague, or hard to see
for holiness had taken flesh
and stood in Nazareth, bold and free.

And still our searching hearts recall
that sacred day in hometown halls:
when The Word stepped off the parchment
and wrote grace upon our walls.

Prayer

Living Word, speak to me. Let Scripture come alive in my heart and let Your truth shape my thoughts, my choices, and my life. Amen.

December 17
The True Vine

> *"I am the true vine, and My Father is the vinedresser."*
> John 15:1, ESV

When Jesus calls Himself the True Vine, He is inviting us into *continual connection*, not occasional visits. A branch can't flourish by checking in once a week; it thrives through constant attachment, quiet dependence, and steady nearness.

This means our spiritual health isn't measured by how *busy* we are for God, but by how *close* we stay to God.

A branch doesn't strain, strategize, or stress to bear fruit. It simply stays connected, and fruit *happens*.

God doesn't applaud spiritual exhaustion. He delights in spiritual abiding.

A friend of mine stepped into church and always assumed God had better things to do than worry about him. So, the remote control and streaming movies became his world, until he ran out of coffee one night.

As he passed the church beside the small market, the nativity scene stood glowing on the lawn. A wooden stable. Twinkling light. And a plastic camel staring at him like it knew my friend's life story.

The following Sunday, curiosity of the church dragged him inside, and the choir sang about a King, who came for the messy, ordinary, and the lost. And my friend sensed a slow crack in the quiet corners of his heart, not thunder, no angels, no glowing star over pew six, just a gentle, undeniable truth settling in; and he wondered, if a nativity scene invited him, and grace welcomed him, could Jesus truly love him?

So again, you know the answer. My friend walked out of that service with hope, not just a bulletin that Sunday.

If you've been feeling worn thin, poured out, or spiritually crispy around the edges, it may not mean you're failing; it may simply mean you're thirsty. (And not for coffee.)

The good news? You don't have to *fix* yourself.

"In *the Garden Vineyards of Kidron Valley*"

Vines curled soft through valley air,
where silent roots drank deep and slow,
and clusters formed not by their push
but by the life that made them grow.

No frantic reach for worth or proof,
no heavy strain to earn or climb
just branches resting in the Vine,
held steady by His love through time.

The valley breeze hummed a quiet truth,
for weary hearts who've tried too long:
growth comes not through anxious hands,
but staying where your soul belongs.

Still vineyards whisper through the years,
with gentle grace in sacred line:
true fruit is born where hearts abide
and live attached to Love Divine.

Prayer

Jesus, keep me close and keep me connected to You, and let Your life flow through every part of who I am. Amen.

December 18
The Resurrection and the Life

> *"Jesus said to her, 'I am the resurrection and the life. Whoever believes in Me, though he die, yet shall he live.'"*
> John 11:25, ESV

These words were not spoken in a peaceful garden or during a celebratory moment; they were spoken beside *a grave*.

Jesus didn't wait for ideal timing or perfect circumstances to reveal His power. He announced the hope of resurrection in the presence of mourners, disappointment, confusion, and tears.

Sometimes we think God's power is best displayed when life looks neat, inspirational, and Instagram-friendly. Or when we post our family Christmas outfits, and our children are smiling. But often, no one sees the crying before the camera snaps.

So, friend, remember: no matter what your family photo truly says about you, remember Jesus still declares life, hope, and forgiveness in Him.

You may have places in your story that feel sealed off:

- dreams that seem buried
- prayers that feel unanswered
- chapters that feel cold and final
- hearts that feel cracked and tired

But Jesus doesn't specialize in resuscitation; He specializes in resurrection.

And resurrection isn't just an Easter headline, it's the Christmas headline, too. It's His identity. It's what He *is*. He is why we celebrate. He is the reason to hark when the angels sing. Wherever Jesus is, death does not get the last word; life does.

So today, whisper this truth into the dusty corners of your soul that Jesus will breathe life into your soul and align your day with His goals.

"At Lazarus' Tomb"

The stone stood firm against the cave,
with silence thick and hope grown thin,
while mourners whispered through their tears,
"Too late... too far... It's over then."

But footsteps stirred the grieving ground,
and Jesus' voice cut through the air
not asking death for permission,
but commanding life to reappear.

Grave clothes rustled with new breath,
the darkness trembled, lost its hold,
for where the Resurrection stands,
no tomb can keep its icy cold.

Still the tomb breathes the truth
for hearts weighed down by fear or strife:
if Jesus calls your name again...
hope rises—and so do you—to life.

Prayer

Lord, breathe life into what feels dead in me. Revive my hope, renew my heart, and restore my joy. Amen.

December 19
The Way, The Truth, and The Life

"Jesus said to him, 'I am the way, and the truth, and the life. No one comes to the Father except through Me.'"
John 14:6, ESV

If life came with a perfect roadmap, we'd all breathe a little easier.

But Jesus didn't hand out GPS coordinates or a step-by-step timetable. He gave us Himself—not a map, but a Guide.

He didn't say, "I'll *show* you the way."

He said, "I *am* the Way."

He didn't say, "I'll *teach* you truth."

He said, "I *am* the Truth."

He didn't say, "I'll *give* you life."

He said, "I *am* the Life."

Following Him isn't about having all the answers; it's about walking with the One who *is* the answer.

So, when confusion fogs the road ahead, or when disappointment whispers that you've made a wrong turn, or when fear insists that you are stuck... stay close to Him. He is the Way through uncertainty, the Truth stronger than every doubt, and the Life deeper than any circumstance.

And sometimes? Life can feel a lot like getting unexpectedly trapped in the middle of a Christmas parade, with lights flashing, people waving, candy flying, and you're not even on a float. You didn't sign up, you didn't rehearse, and you definitely weren't ready for the crowd to watch you inch forward one awkward block at a time in your car.

But even when the noises surround you, slowed by chaos, and wondering how on earth you got there, Jesus knows the route.

He's not just ahead of you, He's with you.

With Jesus, you don't have to fear missing the path because He *is* the path, and He will walk you out with grace, peace, and purpose, even if you're stuck behind the marching band.

"*On the Road to Emmaus*"

Two travelers walked with heavy steps,
their hope bruised thin, their faith worn weak,
when suddenly a Stranger came
and matched their stride, began to speak.

He didn't scold their puzzled hearts,
nor shame their grief or tear-stained views;
He opened Truth like morning light
and stitched their wounds with living news.

And when He broke the evening bread,
their eyes awoke, their spirits stirred
for Life Himself had walked their road,
and every doubt met Living Word.

So, Emmaus whispers still to us
whenever hope seems out of sight:
Walk on. The Way walks with you,
and Truth turns shadows into light.

Prayer

Jesus, lead me in Your way, anchor me in Your truth, and fill me with Your life. Help me follow Your steps. Amen.

December 20
The True Light

"The true light, which gives light to everyone, was coming into the world."
John 1:9, ESV

Light is one of the first gifts God ever spoke into existence, and He hasn't stopped shining it since. But Jesus isn't just a source of light, a spark of light, or a poetic symbol of light; He is the True Light.

There are many "lights" that promise clarity, comfort, identity, or happiness, self-help, approval, achievement, applause, even religion without relationship, but only Jesus illuminates without distortion.

His light doesn't expose to embarrass; it reveals to heal. His light doesn't blind; it guides. His light doesn't fade when life gets dark; it shines brighter.

So, when fear tries to shut off the switch, when anxiety tries to dim your hope, or when lies try to fog your vision, you don't need to fight harder... You need to stay near the Light.

Here's the miracle: His light doesn't just shine around you; it shines in you.

And if you need a visual lesson, hop in the car for a Christmas-lights tour around town. One house will have a glowing nativity scene with angels singing, as if they just finished choir practice in Heaven.

In contrast, the next house looks like Clark Griswold's electricity bill, personally funds the power company. You may even drive by a yard where the snowman leans like it had a long night, and the inflatable Santa looks like he needs prayer and electrolytes.

But here's the funny thing: no matter how tangled, flickering, overdone, or half-deflated those lights are, you still see them. Light wins, always.

And the same Jesus who outshines a billion twinkling bulbs calls you His light-bearer... even on the days you feel more like a dim night-light than a dazzling rooftop display.

"In the Street Markets of Jerusalem"

Lanterns swung through crowded streets,
their flames like whispers in the night,
yet flickered thin with borrowed glow
while shadows lingered out of sight.

But Jesus walked where candles swayed,
and darkness paused beneath His feet,
for True Light doesn't spark and fade
it stands unshaken, whole, complete.

No merchant's glow, no torch or spark
could match the radiance of His grace;
for where He stepped, the night drew back,
and Heaven's dawn lit every space.

Jerusalem's stones remember still
the Light who walked through dust and din:
not just to chase the dark away...
but plant His brilliance deep within.

Prayer

Light of the world, shine in me today. Expose what needs healing, brighten what feels dim, and guide my steps with Your clarity.
Amen.

December 21
The Good News

"And the angel said to them, 'Fear not, for behold, I bring you good news of great joy that will be for all the people.'"
Luke 2:10, ESV

Good news hits different when you've been surrounded by bad news. The shepherds weren't scrolling headlines—their lives *were* hard news.

Long nights. Small pay. Low status. Lonely hillsides. Cold air.

Monotonous routine. And those were the people Heaven chose first.

The Good News didn't debut in the palace, the temple, or the wealthy district; it landed in a field where ordinary, overlooked workers stood watch. Good News means: joy where there wasn't joy, hope where hope felt late, light where light seemed rare, and love where shame felt loud.

And the angel said, "For all the people." Not "for the deserving." Not "for the strong." Not "for the impressive." For all.

So, if today finds you tired, anxious, stressed, unseen, underqualified, over-caffeinated, or somewhere between "trying" and "barely holding on" ... congratulations, the Good News is for you.

And imagine those shepherds when the sky lit up, probably clutching their staffs like makeshift lightsabers, thinking, *"This is it, we're being abducted!"*

But instead of doom, they heard *"Do not fear."*

Instead of criticism, they heard *"Good news of great joy."*

Instead of a to-do list, they received a Savior.

That's the heart of Christmas, God showing up where people least expect Him, with a message so good it makes weary hearts sit up, blink twice, and whisper, "*Wait... this might actually be for me.*"

And friend — it is. Every. Single. Word of it.

"In the Fields Near Shepherds' Watch"

Rough hands gripped staffs beneath the stars,
while breath rose white in midnight air,
no choir hymns, no city lights
just tired souls and subtle prayer.

But then the sky broke wide with song,
and fear gave way to holy thrill,
as Heaven sent its brightest word
to humble hearts on a quiet hill.

Not palace walls nor royal halls
received the first Emmanuel cue
but fields where overlooked hearts stood,
proving Good News begins with you.

Still shepherd winds repeat the sound
in echoes soft across the earth:
that joy can bloom in barren fields...
when Heaven whispers Jesus' birth.

Prayer

Lord, fill me with the joy of Your good news. Let hope rise in me and spill over to everyone I meet today. Amen.

December 22
The Morning Star

"I, Jesus, have sent My angel to testify to you about these things for the churches. I am the root and the descendant of David, the bright morning star."
Revelation 22:16, ESV

The morning star appears in the darkest part of the night, not when dawn has fully arrived, but just before it does. It is Heaven's gentle reminder that light is already on the way, even when it doesn't look like it yet.

Jesus calls Himself the Morning Star, meaning:

- He shows up early
- He shines when things look hopeless
- He signals that darkness is running out of time

You don't have to feel close to a breakthrough for God to be working.

You don't have to see evidence for His promises to be true.

You don't have to pretend it's easy for Him to be faithful.

The Morning Star reminds us that God is not late. He steps into the shadows not to frighten us, but to whisper hope while night is still breathing.

And honestly, this reminds me of when my twin sister, Mel, and I snuck into the living room, when we were in the fourth grade, opened every single gift under the tree, days before Christmas, then retaped them like two undercover elves on a mission.

Christmas morning? Boom—empty tree. We were horrified... and giftless. Talk about hopes and dreams meeting gravity.

All of our presents were hiding in our parents' closet, and they hoped to make a point by strategically putting them away. So, if you're living in a "nothing under the tree" moment, keep watching the horizon. The Morning Star still shines!

"On the Mount of Olives at Dawn"

Before the sunrise brushed the sky
with streaks of gold and whispered grace,
He stood upon the olive hill
where night and hope met face-to-face.

No fanfare broke the fragile dark,
no trumpet split the waking air
just Morning Star in quiet glow
that promised dawn was almost there.

The shadows trembled at His light,
as faith leaned forward, quiet, still,
for victory often starts its march
upon a half-lit, waiting hill.

And Mount of Olives still breathes this truth
for hearts unsure of who they are:
The night is never final, where
He shines — the bright Morning Star.

Prayer

Jesus, shine into my darkest places. Remind me that dawn is coming and that Your light is stronger than any night. Amen.

December 23
Servant King

"Even as the Son of Man came not to be served but to serve, and to give His life as a ransom for many."
Matthew 20:28, ESV

Kings are usually known for being served, wearing crowns, robes, and other regalia, and for having attendants, titles, and all the earthly symbols of importance.

But Jesus turned every royal expectation upside-down. He didn't come demanding a throne... He arrived carrying a towel. His greatness didn't sparkle in the spotlight; it glowed in humility.

He knelt where others would demand honor. He washed feet nobody else wanted to touch. He served those who didn't yet understand Him and loved those who would soon deny Him.

And sometimes His likeness looks a lot like the woman in our church kitchen. The one who plans the Christmas meal weeks in advance, orders the turkey and ham, slices, bastes, seasons, and checks the oven like it's a newborn nursery monitor.

She makes sure the tables are decorated with care, the centerpieces sparkle just enough, the lights twinkle, and the fellowship hall smells like a Hallmark movie with a casserole subplot.

Others bring dishes, yes, and she's grateful. But she's the one who unlocks the door early, arranges the serving line, labels the desserts, wipes the counters, and quietly cleans up long after the last "Merry Christmas!" echoes out the door.

One year, just when she felt the most invisible, the entire church called her to the front. They had handwritten cards, flowers, a gift basket, and a standing ovation that sounded like Heaven's choir rehearsing.

Just so you know, the King whispers to every unseen servant: "Beloved, I saw every moment and none of it was small."

"In the Upper Room"

A basin stood beside the floor,
a silent call no one would claim,
till royalty removed His robe
and dignity bowed without shame.

He knelt where servants usually knelt,
with gentle hands, no pride to bring,
and Heaven gasped with holy awe
for Love was washing like a King.

No throne was needed for His crown,
no trumpet blast, no royal ring;
His greatness shone in whispered grace
the touch of God, the Servant King.

And still that upper room gives voice
to hearts who long for worth again:
true honor lives in humble love,
and greatness wears the towel of Him.

Prayer

Servant King, make my heart like Yours. Teach me to love deeply, serve humbly, and give generously. Amen.

December 24
Indescribable Gift

"Thanks be to God for His inexpressible gift!"
2 Corinthians 9:15, ESV

Some gifts come wrapped in ribbons and bows. Some come with gift receipts tucked inside "just in case." Some make us smile for a moment, and some we forget by February.

But the greatest gift ever given did not come in shiny packaging. He came wrapped in humanity and lay in a manger.

Jesus is the Indescribable Gift because no human language can fully explain: the depth of His grace, the weight of His love, the reach of His mercy, or the power of His presence.

We can try adjectives... beautiful, priceless, holy, life-changing, breathtaking, eternal, yet every word drops short like a pebble trying to describe the ocean.

He is the gift you don't grow out of, don't age out of, don't "finish," and don't ever have to replace.

He fits every heart, every age, every season, every broken piece, every hope, and every tear. And if you've ever watched a preschool Christmas musical, you know what indescribable truly means. That moment when the 6-year-old soloist belts out "Away in a Manger" two octaves too high while waving to his grandma like he just won American Idol—indescribable.

Or when the tiniest toddler dressed as a sheep toddles offstage in search of snacks because the star is too bright and the sheep costume is itchy. Also, indescribable.

Now, if you ever wonder how much God loves you, you don't measure it in words—you measure it in Jesus. So, whisper a thank-you today, not the rushed kind, but the type that rises straight from awe.

Wave to the Savior as you consider his arrival in the manger and sing to him because He is indeed worthy.

"On Golgotha's Hill"

The hill stood stark beneath the sky,
with winds that mourned and shadows spilled,
yet Love climbed high without regret
to gift us grace on Golgotha's hill.

No parchment wrapped His sacrifice,
no satin bow, no festive string,
just crimson mercy dripped like truth
while Heaven hushed on trembling wing.

The nails did not restrain His love
they proved how far His heart would go;
the Gift no words could ever hold
was hung for all the world to know.

And still that hill sings soft through time,
a song too deep for mortal tongue:
the greatest Gift was given there...
while angels wept and hope was sung.

Prayer

Father, thank You for the gift of Jesus. Let gratitude fill me today and reshape the way I see everything around me. Remind me that you are the Indescribable Gift. Amen.

December 25
Christ the Lord

"For unto you is born this day in the city of David, a Savior, who is Christ the Lord."
Luke 2:11, ESV

This is the day all creation leaned toward. Not just a birthday. Not just a manger. A *miracle*. Not just a baby but the Lord of all.

He didn't come because the world was ready. He came because we weren't. He came because we needed rescuing. He came because we needed grace. He came because love refused to stay distant.

He came small enough to hold... yet mighty enough to hold onto us.

Christ the Lord didn't step into the world like a guest; He stepped in as the rightful King, wrapped in humility, handled by human arms, announced by angels, feared by darkness, and adored by Heaven.

And today—right now, in your life—He is still King, not just of Christmas... but of every breath that follows.

So let your soul kneel. Let your heart rise. Let worship ring within you like bells that never dull. Today, we whisper and we proclaim: Christ has come—and Christ is Lord.

And if your heart feels weary, delayed, disappointed, unsure, or halfway between "hallelujah" and "help me," remember, this holy arrival didn't depend on perfect circumstances, cheerful moods, tidy homes, or polished faith.

He came into the mess *on purpose*. Into real life, real problems, real fear, real longing because that's where real redemption shines brightest.

May you celebrate Jesus this Christmas as Heaven leans over the edge of glory, and may you cheer at the hope we have, with every breath.

"At the Empty Tomb"

The morning broke with holy hush,
as the stone rolled back by unseen hands,
and Heaven breathed triumphant air
across the earth and desert sands.

No infant cry, no manger scene,
but resurrected, reigning might
for Christ the Lord stood deathless there,
clothed in forever's flawless light.

And Christmas finds its fullest spark,
beneath that risen, royal sky
for manger's grace becomes complete
where the empty grave meets lifted eyes.

The cradle led to the cross and crown,
so every weary soul may see
His birth began the rescue plan...
His rise sealed our victory.

Forevermore.

Prayer

Christ, my Lord, reign in my heart, direct my steps, and let my worship honor You today and every day. Remind me that you are mighty enough to hold me when my Christmas socks don't match and I rush ahead of You. Amen.

Final Blessing

1. May the **Wonderful Counselor** continue to steady your heart and guide every step you take.

2. May the **Prince of Peace** hush every anxious whisper and breathe calm over your days.

3. May the **Light of the World** shine brightly in your darkest corners and chase away every shadow.

4. May the **Good Shepherd** call your name softly and lead you to green pastures of rest.

5. May the **Bread of Life** nourish your soul with strength this world could never supply.

6. May **Emmanuel** remind you again and again that you are never walking alone.

7. May the **Lamb of God** cover you with grace deep enough to heal every wound.

8. May the **Redeemer** rewrite what you thought was ruined and restore what felt lost.

9. May the **Alpha and Omega** hold your beginnings and endings with perfect care.

10. May the **Savior** draw your heart close and rescue you in ways only He can.

11. May the **King of kings** rule your days with gentleness, justice, and joy.

12. May **The Door** swing wide to lead you into every good thing He has prepared.

13. May **The Vine** keep you rooted, nourished, and bearing fruit in every

season.

14. May the **Rock of Ages** be the firm foundation beneath your trembling moments.

15. May the **Messiah** fulfill His purpose in your story with beauty and strength.

16. May **The Word** speak clearly to you, lighting your path with truth and love.

17. May the **True Vine** draw you close and let His life flow through everything you do.

18. May the **Resurrection and the Life** breathe fresh hope into places you thought were gone.

19. May **The Way, the Truth, and the Life** lead you forward with confidence and clarity.

20. May the **True Light** brighten your outlook and warm every cold place within you.

21. May the **Good News** echo in your heart and spill joy into every conversation you're given.

22. May the **Morning Star** remind you that dawn is coming, even before you see it.

23. May the **Servant King** teach you to love deeply, serve humbly, and walk gently.

24. May the **Indescribable Gift** fill you with gratitude that reshapes how you see your world.

25. And may **Christ the Lord** be your song, your strength, your hope, and your every breath—today and always.

Merry Christmas, beloved.

He is here. He is Lord.

And He loves you.

Books by Pam Kumpe

<u>Annie Grace Kree Chronicles Series</u>
1 Untied Shoelace
2 Unknown Soul
3 Rescue of Undaunted Spirit
4 Unwanted Sidekick
5 Unwavering Hope
6 Unshackled Courage

<u>Other Novels</u>
Rescue at Three Sisters Springs
Looking for Daddy's Girl
Summertime Sprinkler
Where Horses Run Secrets Hide

<u>Devotional</u>
Looking for Daddy's Girl Devotional
See You in the Funny Papers
A Scoop of Inspiration
You Are Not a Typo

<u>Bible Study</u>
Think Outside the Pit Devotional
Think Outside the Pit Workbook

Children
In the Lick of Time
A Goat with a Tote
Hattie Holmes Holds Her Breath
Hattie and Mattie! Oh, They Love the Bunny!
Cranky Camel and the Candy Cane Caper
Cranky the Camel and Max Go to School
Cranky the Camel and Barnyard's Got Talent
Spike's Glow

Rehab Ministry Devotionals
Things I Learned in Jail
From Court to Christ

Homeless Ministry
My View from the Bridge
My View from the Street
My View of the Heart

You Are Lost Series
Book One: The Mystery of Sneaky Pants
Book Two: The Mystery of Sneaky Paws
Book Three: The Mystery of the Sneaky Parrots
Book Four: The Mystery of Sneaky Dill Pickens
Parrots, Pranks, and Prayers Devotional

www.pamkumpe.com

www.ingramcontent.com/pod-product-compliance
Lightning Source LLC
Chambersburg PA
CBHW070634050426
42450CB00011B/3191